The INSIDE GUIDE

CIVICS

Rights and Responsibilities

By Cassie M. Lawton

T0021625

Cavendish Square

New York

Published in 2021 by Cavendish Square Publishing, LLC
243 5th Avenue, Suite 136, New York, NY 10016

Website: cavendishsq.com

This publication represents the opinions and views of the author based on his or her personal experience, knowledge, and research. The information in this book serves as a general guide only. The author and publisher have used their best efforts in preparing this book and disclaim liability rising directly or indirectly from the use and application of this book.

All websites were available and accurate when this book was sent to press.

Portions of this work were originally authored by Leslie Harper and published as *What Are Rights and Responsibilities? (Civics Q&A).* All new material this edition authored by Cassie M. Lawton.

Library of Congress Cataloging-in-Publication Data
Names: Lawton, Cassie M., author.
Title: Rights and responsibilities / by Cassie M. Lawton.
Description: First edition. | New York, NY : Cavendish Square Publishing, [2021] |
Series: The inside guide: civics | Includes index.
Identifiers: LCCN 2020003313 (print) | LCCN 2020003314 (ebook) |
ISBN 9781502657114 (library binding) | ISBN 9781502657091 (paperback) |
ISBN 9781502657107 (set) | ISBN 9781502657121 (ebook)
Subjects: LCSH: Civics–Juvenile literature. |
Political participation–United States–Juvenile literature. |
Citizens–United States–Juvenile literature.
Classification: LCC JK1759 .L39 2021 (print) | LCC JK1759 (ebook) |
DDC 323.0973–dc23
LC record available at https://lccn.loc.gov/2020003313
LC ebook record available at https://lccn.loc.gov/2020003314

Editor: Kristen Susienka
Copy Editor: Nathan Heidelberger
Designer: Tanya Dellaccio

Some of the images in this book illustrate individuals who are models. The depictions do not imply actual situations or events.

CPSIA compliance information: Batch #CS20CSQ: For further information contact Cavendish Square Publishing LLC, New York, New York, at 1-877-980-4450.

Printed in the United States of America

Find us on

CONTENTS

America is a free country, but its citizens still have to obey the rules.

WHAT ARE RIGHTS AND RESPONSIBILITIES?

Chapter One

The United States is often called the "land of the free." This means that the US government doesn't control every part of a citizen's life. However, laws give citizens a **framework** by which to live and detail both their rights and their responsibilities. These laws, rights, and responsibilities are outlined in several important documents and through **legal** systems. Some examples include the US Constitution, which includes the Bill of Rights and several other **amendments**, and state constitutions.

Citizens are people who are legally recognized as being part of a country. Some people become citizens by being born in a country or by having parents who are citizens of the country. Others move to a country and go through a series of steps to become citizens there. Citizens make up the majority of the population in most countries, and citizens in every country deserve to be treated well. Their rights are important. Citizens also have responsibilities that help their country function well.

A Closer Look

A right is something that everyone should be able to do. In the United States, citizens have some very important rights. They can choose their own religion and defend themselves if they're charged with a crime. They can protest, or speak out against, the government if they disagree with certain issues. In some countries, people can't do these things without getting in trouble.

Citizens also have important responsibilities. A responsibility is something that a person must do. Obeying the laws may be our most important responsibility as citizens. Laws are rules for what we can and can't do. Many of them keep us safe. When people obey laws, it's easier for everyone to live together peacefully. When everyone acts as a responsible citizen, we can all enjoy our rights!

Sometimes, it's hard to understand what's a right and what's a responsibility.

The Bill of Rights

The US Constitution lays out some of the country's main laws. It also set up the structure for how the government works. It was written after the American Revolution, which took place from 1775 to 1783. Then, the United States was a new country. The men who wrote the Constitution wanted all 13 original states to sign and ratify, or approve, it. The leaders in some states saw a problem, though. They thought the Constitution gave the US government a lot of power but didn't grant citizens enough rights.

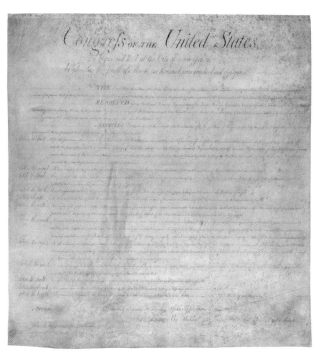

Shown here is the Bill of Rights—the first 10 amendments to the Constitution.

The Bill of Rights was created to fix this problem. At first, 17 changes to the Constitution were suggested. Later, that number was lowered to 12. In the end, 10 amendments were officially added to the Constitution. These became the Bill of Rights. These amendments promise people certain rights that can't be taken away.

Fast Fact

The US Constitution divides the government into three branches: legislative, executive, and judicial. The legislative branch creates laws, the executive branch carries out laws, and the judicial branch interprets laws.

The American people have the right to protest.

The First Amendment's Role

Many of the rights that citizens value most in the United States are in the First Amendment. This amendment says that the government can't force people to belong to a certain religion. It also gives people the right to speak out against things they don't agree with. This is often called freedom of speech. The right to free speech also applies to the press, such as newspapers, magazines, and internet sites.

The First Amendment also gives people the right to assemble, or meet together peacefully in groups. People have used this right to publicly protest laws that they think are unfair. Protests have been important steps in gaining rights for people in the United States and around the world.

Fast Fact

Many rights, such as freedom of speech and religion, are promised to all people in the United States, not just to US citizens. However, only US citizens have the right to vote in national elections.

FIGHTING FOR THEIR RIGHTS

Throughout much of US history, African Americans were treated unfairly because their race was different from the race of the white people in power. This treatment is called discrimination. Until 1865, many African Americans were slaves on **plantations** in the South. After the American Civil War, the Constitution was changed so they were freed from slavery and able to enjoy other rights as citizens, but they still weren't treated equally in many states. They had different places to eat and drink, different places to go to school, and different places to sit on city buses.

In the 1950s and 1960s, things began to change. People began to protest, demanding the US government pay attention and treat African Americans equally. This struggle is often called the civil rights movement.

Many important leaders appeared during this time, such as Rosa Parks, Martin Luther King Jr., and John Lewis. They all worked hard to make the country a better place.

In the 1960s, African Americans marched in many states, demanding equal rights.

The Founding Fathers worked to protect the rights of US citizens.

AMENDMENTS AND RIGHTS

Amendments are important parts of the Constitution. They've helped the Constitution change as times have changed. Many amendments have granted rights to people who didn't have certain rights when the Constitution was written. Throughout history, there have been many important amendments related to the rights of citizens. State governments also have constitutions and amendments that deal with these issues.

Voting Rights Amendments

The right to vote is an important part of being a citizen in the United States. Many people who serve in government are elected. This includes the US president, state governors, city council members, and many others. In an election, each person casts a vote for a candidate. Usually, the candidate with the most votes wins.

Fast Fact

As of early 2020, the US Constitution has had 27 amendments added since it was written.

Native Americans were one of the last groups of people to be allowed to vote in the United States.

Fast Fact

Before the Snyder Act was passed in 1924, Native Americans weren't considered US citizens, and therefore they weren't allowed to vote. Even after they gained citizenship, Native Americans continued to have trouble voting in many states. Utah was the last US state to promise voting rights to Native Americans, in 1962.

For a long time, African Americans, women, and others were not allowed to vote. They fought for many years to have their voices heard by the government. Eventually, amendments were passed to grant voting rights to these groups. These amendments weren't all passed at once, though. For example, the 15th Amendment, passed in 1870, says that citizens can't be prevented from voting based on their race. This opened the door for African American men to vote. Then, in 1920, the 19th Amendment extended voting rights to women.

Despite amendments like these, many states still found ways to discriminate against different groups. Additional laws were needed to strengthen people's voting rights. One example is the Voting Rights Act of 1965, which helped make sure all African Americans could vote in all states.

Today, if you want to vote in US elections, you must be a US citizen and be at least 18 years old. Elections for different offices happen at the local, state, and **federal** levels. It's important to exercise your right to vote in all elections when you're old enough. Voting is not just a right. It's an important responsibility too. In an election, every vote matters!

Amendments That Protect Us

Everyone has legal rights, and some amendments are meant to protect them. For example, the Fourth through Seventh Amendments say how people should be treated when **accused** of crimes. These amendments try to make the process as fair as possible. They say that police can't come into your home without permission (called a warrant). They give people the right to a **jury trial**, a lawyer, and many other protections.

The Eighth Amendment deals with what happens when someone is found guilty of a crime. It forbids "cruel and unusual punishments." Today, people disagree about what that means. Some people argue that it means people can't be put to death as punishment for a crime, but others think

The Fourth Amendment says police officers need a warrant to enter your home.

Fast Fact

Americans have the right to bear arms, or own weapons. This is granted in the Second Amendment.

the death penalty is allowed under the amendment. Most agree that the amendment doesn't allow for torture as a punishment for a crime.

The people who wrote the Constitution knew they couldn't think of everything, however. The Ninth Amendment says that just because a right isn't listed, that doesn't mean people don't have it. The 10th Amendment adds that those powers not assigned to the federal government by the Constitution belong instead to state governments or to the people. Thus, states also have their own laws and expectations for citizens.

The rights citizens are granted through amendments and other laws come with responsibilities. Keep reading to learn about those!

THE SUPREME COURT

A group of federal judges called the Supreme Court decides if laws are in line with the Constitution. They help shape the meaning of new laws, do away with **unconstitutional** laws, and hear cases about different rights. The US presidents choose the Supreme Court judges, called justices. The Senate approves them. Each justice serves for life or until they decide to retire. All justices work together to make decisions about laws and the Constitution. They hear many cases each year, and many cases involve citizens' rights. For example, the Supreme Court has heard cases about the right to marriage equality and the right for children of all races to have an equal education. Their rulings about civil rights have made the United States a more equal place.

Fast Fact

In 1954, the Supreme Court case called *Brown v. Board of Education* focused on equality in education.

There are nine judges, called justices, on the Supreme Court.

All US citizens 18 years and older can serve on a jury. They have to promise, or take an oath, to be fair and honest.

JURIES AND TAXES

The United States grants rights and assigns responsibilities to everyone living there. People who carry out their responsibilities and follow the laws are good citizens.

What's Jury Duty?

Jury service, often called jury duty, is when a person goes to a court during a trial and sits on a jury. The jury is the group of people who decide if a person is guilty of a crime.

People who serve on juries listen to the facts of the case. When all the facts have been given, they must decide who's telling the truth and what the facts mean. The jury listens closely to both sides of a case before they make a decision.

Jury duty is a very important responsibility. If people didn't serve on juries, those who are accused of crimes could not exercise their right to a jury trial.

Any US citizen 18 years and older living in the United States can be on a jury. However, they must first be selected. The jury selection process depends on where you live and what court cases need jury members. A citizen called for jury duty first receives a **summons** in the mail. Then, they go to a court to be selected. During the selection process, a person is asked a series of questions. Depending on their answers, they might get a spot on the jury. Lawyers involved in the trial select people who they think will make good judgments. It's also good to have a **diverse** jury to represent all parts of a community. Some people serve on juries many times in their lives. Other people are never selected!

People who serve on a jury are called jurors. Juries are made up of different members of a community.

Fast Fact

In most criminal cases, all members of a jury must agree on the decision, or verdict, they give to the court. Criminal cases concern serious issues like murder, stealing, or drugs. The person who has committed the crime faces time in jail or even death if the crime is serious enough and they're proven guilty.

Jury Duty Process

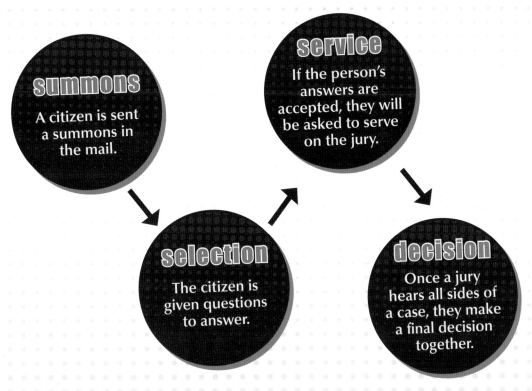

summons
A citizen is sent a summons in the mail.

selection
The citizen is given questions to answer.

service
If the person's answers are accepted, they will be asked to serve on the jury.

decision
Once a jury hears all sides of a case, they make a final decision together.

What Are Taxes?

Taxes have been part of American life since before the American Revolution. Today, they remain an important part of society. Paying taxes is a great responsibility that should be taken seriously.

A tax is money that a person pays to the government. People pay taxes on money they earn through their jobs. The government then uses this money to pay for many important parts of a community, such as public schools, libraries, firefighters, and police officers.

There are also taxes related to buying goods. A sales tax is collected when a person buys things. This tax is determined by states and cities.

Taxes are amounts of money taken from people that are used to help the country or local community.

Often, the sales tax isn't included in the displayed price of an item. Instead, it's added on later. However, this isn't the case in some states and in other countries.

Every year, the government requires people to submit paperwork that lists their taxes. This is called filing your taxes. All people living in the United States must file their taxes, even if they aren't US citizens. People who don't file taxes can get in big trouble and go to jail. Americans living in another country must also file their taxes with the US government.

Fast Fact

In the United States, Tax Day is typically on April 15. This is the day by which everyone must file their taxes.

People who help others file their taxes are called accountants.

WHERE DO YOUR TAXES GO?

Taxes are a major responsibility for people in the United States, but what are they used for? The federal government's Internal Revenue Service (IRS) receives all federal taxes. The US Congress decides what to do with the tax money. They do this by passing a budget, which divides the money between different federal programs. One of the biggest programs is Social Security, which provides money each month for the elderly and disabled. Other programs provide health care for elderly and **low-income** people. Taxes pay for the US military and other measures that help keep the country safe. They also help pay for medical research and many other useful things.

State and local governments collect their own taxes to pay for services in their communities. Examples are helping run public schools and maintaining local roads and parks. It might seem **frustrating** that people have to pay money to the government, but taxes benefit people all around the country.

The Internal Revenue Service receives all federal taxes every year. It also gives out **tax refunds**.

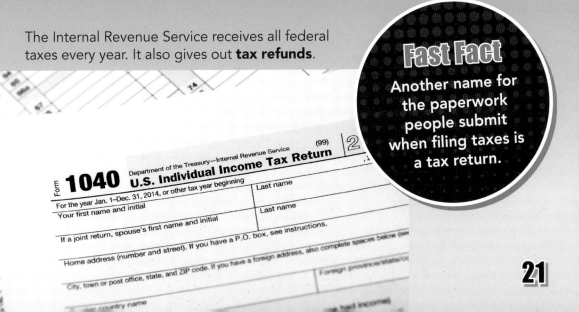

Fast Fact

Another name for the paperwork people submit when filing taxes is a tax return.

In the United States, people have the right to gather in groups, but they have a responsibility to do so peacefully.

TAKING ACTION TODAY

It's important to know your responsibilities and your rights. The United States offers the people who live there many rights, including the right to freely express feelings and opinions. Throughout history, this right has helped many citizens speak out and get other rights they didn't have before. The rights we enjoy in the United States help keep our country fair. The responsibilities we have are strongly connected to those rights.

Rights Around the World

Countries around the world offer different rights to their citizens to create a good, functioning society. In the United States, rights are important parts of life. They help people feel safe and **appreciated**. They also help people if they're in trouble.

It's important to remember that not all rights are the same in every country. If you move to or travel to another country, be sure to understand what your rights are when you go there. Many rights are the same, but some are different. For example, in some countries, people don't have the right to wear whatever they want. They must follow certain rules and keep certain body parts covered. In other countries, protesting against the government is not allowed.

It's important for people visiting another country to understand and follow that country's rules.

Fast Fact

Many laws of other countries are found in their constitutions. Reading a country's constitution and understanding its laws is important to do before traveling to a new place.

What Can You Do?

We all have a responsibility be informed and **model** citizens. We can do this by following the laws of our city, state, and country. We can also help others understand and follow them.

You may be too young to do some of the things that adults do, such as vote or serve in the military. However, there are many ways that kids can be responsible community members. First, work to help others and the community in which you live. Try planning a food drive at your school, cleaning up litter in a park, or finding other ways to volunteer in your community, such as at a library or animal shelter. You can also ask your parents to help you find a group in your community that you can join. One example is the Boy Scouts or Girl Scouts. Helping through a community organization can bring you lots of joy, give you new skills, and help you pratice being a responsible citizen.

Fast Fact

The Boy and Girl Scouts of America have a motto, or saying: "Be prepared." It means members should take the skills they learn and be ready to use them when needed. These words help members be aware of their community and help out in all situations.

Helping in your community is one way to show you're a responsible citizen.

You can study the US Constitution in school and learn about the different rules and laws followed in the United States. Research laws in your community, city, or state. Also, learn more about what it means to be responsible. Help adults who can vote make good decisions and vote for people and laws that will help others. Talking to law enforcement officers, like police officers, can also give you a better understanding of what it means to be a responsible citizen.

These are documents that show someone is a US citizen.

Fast Fact

Some countries around the world require all citizens of a certain age to spend time serving in the military. The United States has all men register to join the military in an emergency situation, but professional soldiers make their own decisions to join the military.

A GLOBAL CITIZEN

Wherever you live or travel, remember you are a citizen of the world too. It's important to be a responsible citizen of the world. Being a good global citizen means treating others in different countries with respect. Gaining an understanding of others is an important part of being a global citizen too. It's important to learn about other **cultures** and their ways of life. Gestures we might think are friendly might be rude to people in other countries. Also remember that if you travel, what you say and do is a reflection of your country. People who might not know others from your country might think all people act the way you do. If you act nicely, you will paint yourself and your country in a good light.

People from other cultures have the right to be respected.

TIMELINE

Key Amendments in US History

1791
The First Amendment grants freedom of speech, religion, and the press.

1868
The 14th Amendment grants citizenship to freed slaves.

1870
The 15th Amendment gives all men, regardless of race, the right to vote.

1920
The 19th Amendment grants women the right to vote.

1971
The 26th Amendment sets the voting age at 18.

Sixty-sixth Congress of the United States of America;

At the First Session,

Begun and held at the City of Washington on Monday, the nineteenth day of May, one thousand nine hundred and nineteen.

JOINT RESOLUTION

Proposing an amendment to the Constitution extending the right of suffrage to women.

1. What's the difference between a right and a responsibility? Why do they matter today?

2. Why are amendments important? How can they help citizens? Name some that have helped others in the past.

3. Imagine being on a jury. How would you practice being a good citizen in a courtroom?

4. What are some steps you can take to practice responsibility in your community?

accuse: To place blame for a wrongdoing on someone.

amendment: An addition or change to the Constitution.

appreciate: To acknowledge and thank someone for actions or deeds they've done.

culture: The beliefs, practices, and ways of life of a group of people.

diverse: Made up of people from many different backgrounds.

federal: Relating to the government of a whole country rather than an individual city or state.

framework: A structure or outline.

frustrating: Causing feelings of anger or annoyance because something is upsetting or unfair.

jury trial: A process in which a group of people is chosen to make a decision in a court case based on the facts given to them.

legal: Relating to the law.

low-income: Making little money at a job, which can lead to not being able to afford many goods.

model: Serving as an example to others.

plantation: A large farm in the southern United States, generally before and during the American Civil War.

summons: A call, received in the mail, for jury duty.

tax refund: Money returned by the IRS to a citizen who has overpaid taxes during a year.

unconstitutional: Going against the Constitution.

Books

Barcella, Laura. *Know Your Rights!: A Modern Kid's Guide to the American Constitution*. New York, NY: Sterling Children's Books, 2018.

Bartoletti, Susan Campbell. *How Women Won the Vote*. New York, NY: HarperCollins, 2020.

Leavitt, Amie Jane. *The Bill of Rights in Translation: What It Really Means*. North Mankato, MN: Capstone Press, 2018.

Websites

Amendments to the US Constitution
www.britannica.com/topic/list-of-amendments-to-the-U-S-Constitution-1787122
This *Encyclopedia Britannica* article explains all of the amendments to the US Constitution.

Learn About Jury Service
www.uscourts.gov/services-forms/jury-service/learn-about-jury-service
The US court system website provides information about jury duty, the selection process, and what to expect in the event a citizen is selected.

National Constitution Center
constitutioncenter.org
The National Constitution Center gives information about the US Constitution, including facts, history, and an interactive document to explore.